The Meeting Black Belt™

Run Meetings People Can't Wait to Attend

Soulaima Gourani

The Meeting Black Belt™

First published Soulaima Gourani - 2024

Copyright © 2024 Soulaima Gourani

All rights reserved. No part of this publication may be copied or reproduced in any form, by any means, electronic or otherwise, without prior consent from the copyright owner and publisher of this book.

First edition

Table of Contents

Table of Contents 3

Introduction 4

Chapter 1: Defining Meeting Intelligence (MQ) 7

Chapter 2: The Future of Work and Meeting Expectations 29

Chapter 3: Fostering Engagement - Unlocking the Power of Participation 36

Chapter 4: Purpose-Driven Meetings - Avoiding Timewasters 43

Chapter 5: The Role of Leadership in Shaping Meeting Culture 48

Chapter 6: Time Management in Meetings - Mastering the Clock 60

Chapter 7: The Impact of Meeting Culture on Employee Retention 66

Chapter 8: Asynchronous Communication - A Game-Changer for the Hybrid Era 75

Chapter 9: Leveraging Technology to Enhance Meeting Intelligence 82

Chapter 10: Frameworks for Meeting Success - Practical Tools for Leaders 84

Chapter 11: Your Role in Shaping the Future of Meetings 87

Chapter 12: Conclusion - Your Journey to Master Meeting Intelligence (MQ) 88

Introduction

*By Soulaima Gourani, globally recognized author, keynote speaker and expert in leadership, inclusion, technology, and the future of work. She is the Founder of Happioh - an AI **spam filter for meetings that won** the AI & Data category at the 7th Annual Product Awards 2024, selected by leaders from Amazon, Bank of America, and S&P Global, Capgemini, and Mighty Capital.*

Anyone who knows me knows how much I can't stand bad meetings. Bad meetings don't just kill time; they drain energy, stifle creativity, and slowly drive everyone a little nuts! The wild part? Most people are handed a company email and access to a calendar on day one, and they're off to the races, running meetings like they're driving a car without a license. No training, no structure, just a crash course in "invite everyone" and hope for the best. Over time, old habits from past roles creep in, and before you know it, meetings become dreaded time sinks instead of powerful tools. After years in the trenches of corporate meeting culture (trust me, I've seen it all), I'm on a mission to turn meetings into something you actually look forward to - and even use as a competitive advantage - The Meeting Black Belt™, a skill worthy on your CV!

I know firsthand how mastering GREAT meetings can change your life.

As a 7th-grade school dropout, I built my career in the boardrooms and meeting rooms of some of the world's biggest companies. Meetings were where I learned to connect, persuade, and lead. These skills opened doors I never imagined possible.

Mastering meetings isn't just a nice-to-have skill; it's a strategic advantage. Just like athletes rigorously train to reach peak performance, professionals need to approach meetings as a high-stakes game because, for many, that's exactly what it is. Meetings are where ideas are born, partnerships are forged, and careers are made. When you walk into a room prepared, skilled, and ready to lead, you're not just participating, you're playing to win.

AI is making meetings faster, more efficient, and often more productive. But when it comes to what truly matters in a meeting, building trust, resolving conflict, inspiring people, none of this is about the tools. It's about the people in the room.

Think about it. The moments that leave a lasting impact in any meeting are rarely about logistics or data points. They're about someone taking the time to remember your name, genuinely listening, or sharing a personal insight that connects with you on a deeper level. These are the human touches that build trust, create partnerships, and drive collaboration forward.

We're at a moment in history where technology can handle much of the *how*. AI can summarize, track tasks, and even guide some of the structure. But the magic of leadership lies in the *why* and the *who*. It's the ability to connect, to inspire, to align people behind a shared purpose, and that will always be human work. The good news? Technology isn't here to replace us; it's here to amplify what makes us great. AI will take care of the mundane so we can focus on what matters, relationships, creativity, bold ideas. That's where real leadership lives.

In a world increasingly shaped by automation, the leaders who stand out will be the ones who lean into what only humans can do. They'll be the ones who read the room, who know when to pause for a story, who bring out the best in people. These aren't skills you can download or automate - they're the skills that make us human.

The future of meetings isn't just efficient - it's transformative. It's about combining technology's capabilities with timeless leadership traits: empathy, intuition, and connection. The leaders who embrace this balance will not only navigate the future but define it.

Enjoy!

Soulaima Gourani

Chapter 1: Defining Meeting Intelligence (MQ)

My journey proves that anyone can develop Meeting Intelligence (MQ) and leverage it to transform their career. It's not just about showing up; it's about showing up ready, being present, and treating every meeting like a chance to perform at your best.

Meetings are more than routine gatherings; they're where strategy meets action, where ideas clash, and where the next big opportunity often reveals itself. Each meeting is a stage, a performance, and a unique chance to influence outcomes. When you enter with that mindset, your presence alone can command attention, and your input becomes truly impactful.

We spend countless hours perfecting skills like public speaking or project management, but few realize that Meeting Intelligence (MQ) is the hidden key that separates leaders from followers. Most career-defining moments unfold in meetings.

By treating each meeting as a space to be prepared, persuasive, and strategic, you unlock career-changing potential. A great meeting isn't just about ticking off agenda items; it's about creating opportunities. It's where alliances are built, insights are gained, and decisions are influenced. Every minute invested in honing your meeting skills can yield exponential returns, transforming each meeting into a platform for growth and influence.

Meetings are the crucible of leadership. It's where people decide who they trust, who they respect, and who they want to follow. Mastering your meeting skills - whether through listening, sharing insights, or effective follow-ups—positions you as someone who knows how to lead. After all, meetings are a concentrated exercise in influence, a microcosm of how you communicate, listen, and navigate dynamics. Each one is an opportunity to refine your brand as a leader, to go beyond making an impression and start making an impact. When you take meetings seriously and treat them as catalysts for change, you elevate yourself and set a new standard for those around you.

With discipline, you can turn this into a game-changing skill that sets you apart. Remember, every great leader, innovator, and decision-maker has mastered the art of the meeting. Now it's your turn to take this sport seriously, sharpen your MQ, and watch new doors open.

The future of work must become more human-centric to address the growing problem of loneliness. With remote work becoming the norm, constant team changes, and the rise of gig work, lasting relationships are on the decline. We're no longer experiencing the workplace as a familial environment, leaving many individuals feeling isolated.

Adding to this, AI is increasingly taking over managerial tasks, including performance feedback and decision-making.

Some companies are even reshaping their organizational structures, focusing less on middle management and more on leveraging AI for hiring, development, and dismissals. Research indicates that many organizations, especially in tech, are experimenting with streamlining management layers, shifting more responsibilities to AI tools to enhance efficiency. The rapid pace of AI development will present ongoing challenges. With the technology evolving faster than anticipated, businesses must remain vigilant, ensuring that human oversight remains a key component of AI-powered processes. We as leaders must not only understand AI tools but also be able to explain the rationale behind our decisions.

Meetings, therefore, need to shift focus. Instead of being transactional, they should be treated as human-centered spaces - enabling connection, respect, and productive collaboration. A strong framework for this is **PERMA**, a model built on:

- **P**ersonal connections: Fostering authentic interactions
- **E**ngagement: Ensuring active participation
- **R**elationships: Strengthening collaboration and teamwork
- **M**eaningful: Be relevant for people's work
- **A**chievement: Celebrating progress and results

When these elements are woven into meetings, they become more than routine check-ins or long endless discussions and time wasters and soul crushers - they become essential tools for maintaining well-being, trust, and purpose in the workplace. By adopting such intentional approaches, organizations can balance technology with human connection, ensuring AI serves to complement - not replace - meaningful interpersonal engagement.

People often remark that my meetings are among the most effective they've attended. Why? Because they're designed with a clear purpose, well-timed, and well moderated. While I may have a knack for this, it's my system that drives results.

Here's the process: I don't join meetings unprepared. Every participant gets a pre-meeting note from me, think of it as a "pre-cap" that includes context and purpose, in a brief 2-minute read. This small investment ensures everyone comes prepared, making our time together exponentially more valuable.

In the meeting, I capture insights and immediately distil them into action items, shared in a concise post-meeting recap. While automated transcriptions can capture a lot, a distilled, 200-300 character recap is what drives action.

I track every decision and follow up rigorously, closing the loop and ensuring nothing slips through the cracks.

It's a system that turns meetings into high-impact meetings. Information flows efficiently, accountability is clear, and outcomes are achieved consistently. It's a straightforward process, but one that keeps me at the center of knowledge and momentum. Simple, efficient, effective.

Once you establish a solid system, it liberates your energy for what really drives success - focusing on people, leadership, and emotional intelligence. These are the levers that move people to take action, innovate, and share insights freely. Systems handle the operational details so you can invest in the human dynamics that propel an organization forward. That's where the real breakthroughs happen when you're focused less on the mechanics and more on creating an environment where ideas and execution thrive.

Professor Thomas Roulet's wisdom inspires me: Leadership in 2030 will be like following a recipe. While core ingredients -

like vision, motivation, and risk-taking - remain essential, success will depend on the ability to adapt these elements to different contexts.

In a world increasingly shaped by isolation and uncertainty, leaders must focus on *individualized consideration* - recognizing and valuing people as individuals, not just as part of the collective. With AI and instability reshaping workplaces, prioritizing mental health and fostering genuine connections with teams is more critical than ever. Additionally, leaders need creativity, flexibility, and a resilient narrative that can withstand uncertainty. Leadership in the current context cannot avoid being human centered.

Here's an original bio from someone on Elpha.com. She's a total meeting wizard. You can feel her power and drive, right? Let her vibe inspire you:

About:

"I am the person that keeps meetings on task, clarifies next steps, and gets stuff done. I have always been that way. My organization and self-motivation apply to all aspects of my life and is always one of my employers' top praises of me."

I know that taking control of your calendar can feel daunting, especially when it means asking colleagues to improve their meeting invites, so you have the details you need to make informed decisions. If you're struggling to decide which meetings to prioritize, try this litmus test: *Will this meeting bring me closer to—or further from—my professional and personal goals?*

Don't be afraid to set high standards. Ironically, the longer you work with people, the less structured their invites may become, often leading to meetings that feel unprepared or even rushed. And when you suggest improvements, some may take it personally, thinking, "It's just me, your colleague." However, maintaining a "tight ship" with your calendar is essential. After all, your time is valuable, and every meeting should be purposeful.

I want team members who are skilled meeting-makers, those who have a "black belt" in running effective, high-quality meetings. **Be that person**. It's a valuable asset, much like holding a driver's license. Knowing how to run a productive, impactful meeting isn't just a nice-to-have; it's a critical skill that stands out in any team!

Remember that meeting styles are shaped by a rich mix of cultures, genders, and generational preferences, and these differences can profoundly impact meeting dynamics. Having led meetings in over 50 countries, I've seen firsthand how expectations vary around the world. In places like Finland and Japan, for instance, silence is often valued; people tend to listen deeply and speak only after thoughtful consideration, which may come across as reserved to those from more expressive cultures. Contrast that with France, Italy, and MENA regions, where lively exchanges and passionate voices are the norm—louder volumes don't signal anger but enthusiasm and engagement.

Gender also plays a role in meeting dynamics. Research shows that men tend to speak more and are often more assertive or prone to interrupt, while women may lean toward collaborative and inclusive communication styles. Unfortunately, assertive women can sometimes face unfair labels, which can discourage participation and affect the tone of meetings. Also be aware of gender-neutral language. Instead, of saying "Greetings ladies and gentlemen". Try "Greetings everyone" or just "hi team".

Cultural nuances further shape these preferences. For example, many Asian cultures value hierarchy and may expect senior voices to lead discussions, whereas Western cultures, particularly in the U.S., often encourage open contributions across all levels. Understanding these nuanced differences - whether regional, gender-based, or generational - can make meetings more inclusive and effective. When we tailor our approach to the unique cultural and personal dynamics of our team, we foster an environment where everyone can contribute meaningfully, ensuring our meetings aren't just productive but also respectful and engaging.

The DNA of a Great Meeting

Meetings aren't the problem - it's how we run them. When managed effectively, meetings don't just work; they elevate people and organizations, driving both personal growth and business success!

Poorly run meetings don't just waste time - they erode team morale and create a ripple of disengagement. 70% of employees believe their job satisfaction would improve if they attended fewer meetings. It's completely valid to hate meetings if you don't know that it's possible to design them to be effective.

If you repeatedly host ineffective meetings, you're not just losing time; you're losing trust and damaging your reputation as a leader. And trust me - people remember your low-quality meetings. Learn how to run a great meeting and your career will improve dramatically. Since the 1990s, I've been in the trenches of corporate life, clocking thousands of hours in meetings that, let's face it, often had more fluff than substance. Throughout my corporate career, meetings stretched across the entire day - lunches with beer and cigarettes, followed by long dinner nights with drinks. Back then, workplace dynamics were grueling. It was common for women to be reduced to note-takers, and expectations for long hours were the norm.

There were times I'd leave the office but leave my jacket on the chair and the desk light on - just to give the appearance I was still working. The more hours you put in, the more dedicated you were perceived to be. I still carry some PTSD from those days! This topic isn't just theoretical. It's personal.

Let's address the elephant in the room: Most people hate meetings - except those who do them for a living. In the words of Derek Thompson, white-collar work has morphed into a perpetual cycle of meetings. This shift underscores a troubling trend: meetings have become not just tools for collaboration, but mechanisms for survival. The result? Endless communication that stalls innovation and stifles deep, meaningful work.

Many employees feel more like full-time meeting attendees than productive professionals, averaging 3 to 5 meetings a day. The advice to "just decline meetings" might sound nice in theory, but the reality is far more complex. Many employees serve as critical information bridges - if they miss a meeting, they lose essential context, which leads to scrambling later to catch up. The challenge is clear: organizations must rethink their meeting structures to reduce overload while still ensuring that crucial information flows smoothly and educate teams better how to host high quality meetings that are worth people's time.

How many endless meetings have I sat through that could've been an email? I built my career by learning how to master meetings - understanding not just the mechanics, but the subtle art of driving conversations that matter. To have a better meeting culture is a team effort. Use meetings for the things that you can't do asynchronously.

I started out as a 7th-grade dropout, but my ability to navigate meetings effectively propelled me forward. From working with giants like Maersk and HP to securing partnerships with Microsoft, I've lived the power of meetings done right. Those meeting skills laid the foundation for my entrepreneurial journey, eventually leading to Happioh Inc. - the best AI product of 2024, winning with 500,000 votes from Product That Counts.

Together with Thomas Roulet, a leading academic mind, we've poured years of experience and insights into developing the concept of Meeting Intelligence (MQ) - the framework for meetings that get things done. Now, as someone who has been at the forefront of multiple startups and facilitated workshops across industries, I can tell you this: Meetings are the new battleground for productivity. Master them, and you master your career. This chapter will introduce the DNA of a great meeting - the building blocks of Meeting Intelligence (MQ).

When leaders know how to lead great meetings, there's less time wasted and less frustration. We have more energy to do the work that matters, realize our full potential, and do great things.

Justin Rosenstein

What Exactly Is Meeting Intelligence (MQ)?

In a world where AI and virtual tools are redefining communication, it's easy to forget one fundamental truth: meaningful relationships are built face-to-face. According to Harvard, 95% of professionals agree that in-person meetings are essential for fostering long-term relationships.

Yale research goes a step further, showing that virtual meetings simply don't engage the brain the same way. There's something irreplaceable about eye contact, shared presence, and the trust that begins forming within minutes. While AI can streamline communication, automate workflows, and facilitate networking, it can't replicate the depth of connection that comes from being in the same room. This is where Meeting Intelligence (MQ) becomes a strategic advantage. The leaders who master MQ understand that meetings aren't just operational touchpoints - they're moments to inspire, align, and build trust. In-person meetings, when run well, spark creativity, accelerate decision-making, and unlock collaboration in ways that virtual interactions can't. It's not about rejecting technology - it's about knowing when human connection makes the difference. Leaders who grasp this nuance - and elevate their MQ - will attract better talent, forge stronger partnerships, and ultimately, win the future.

In my recent Forbes article, I explored the art of meaningful conversations - a piece that struck a chord and quickly went viral. Why? Because today, we've lost the ability to engage in balanced, meaningful dialogue. As our collective EQ declines and attention spans shorten, these skills are becoming rarer - and more valuable.

This gap is especially visible with Generation Z and Generation Alpha, who face increasing challenges connecting across generations. They are growing up in a world dominated by rapid-fire communication and fragmented interactions, where in-person conversations feel more daunting than ever. And meetings, especially, suffer from this disconnect. According to recent reports, a significant reason why some Gen Z employees are getting fired is due to perceived deficiencies in their communication skills, often attributed to their heavy reliance on digital communication like texting and social media, which can lead to misunderstandings in professional settings requiring face-to-face interactions, clear articulation, and proper etiquette.

- *Digital native gap:* Growing up primarily on digital platforms can lead to challenges in traditional communication methods like phone calls, in-person meetings, and formal email writing.
- *Informal language and tone:* The casual language used in online communication can sometimes translate into unprofessional communication in the workplace.

- *Lack of active listening skills:* Over-reliance on texting can lead to less developed active listening skills, which are crucial in professional settings.
- *Feedback interpretation issues*: Gen Z may struggle to interpret constructive criticism, especially when delivered in a traditional manner, leading to misunderstandings.

The leaders who excel at Meeting Intelligence - who understand how to design meetings that foster real connection, trust, and collaboration - will have a distinct competitive advantage.

Meetings are not just operational checkpoints - they are platforms for meaningful conversations that build trust, foster collaboration, and shape culture. Much like mastering the art of conversation, meeting intelligence (MQ) is about more than just structured agendas and time management - it's about creating environments where real connection can thrive.

At the core of both great conversations and effective meetings is the ability to listen actively, engage meaningfully, and foster openness. Leaders who excel in meetings understand that their goal is not simply to convey information but to create dialogue - to unlock new ideas, resolve conflicts, and inspire action. Just as conversations build personal relationships, well-run meetings build organizational trust and alignment.

Ever wonder why some meetings trigger anxiety before they even begin? It's not just the content of the meeting but how it's framed that sets the tone. I've seen this firsthand how employees admitted they dreaded surprise meetings or unplanned one-on-ones - associating them with bad news, blame, or even terminations.

This begs the question: Are we unknowingly creating this same sense of dread within our teams? A simple shift in how we structure, and name meetings can change everything. Imagine sending out meeting invites labeled 'Good News,' 'New Ideas,' or 'Positive Feedback.' These small, intentional changes signal positivity and openness, reducing unnecessary anxiety and fostering a more supportive work culture. The best leaders understand that meetings are about more than just logistics - they are opportunities to build trust and strengthen relationships!

What Sets Great Meetings Apart?

1. *Listening with Intent:* In meetings, leaders must be present and listen beyond words - reading between the lines, recognizing non-verbal cues, and giving space for participants to express themselves. This kind of active listening signals respect and encourages openness, much like a deep conversation would.
2. *Creating Psychological Safety:* Just as a meaningful conversation depends on trust, effective meetings rely on psychological safety. Participants must feel comfortable sharing bold ideas without fear of judgment. Leaders with high MQ intentionally create spaces for diverse perspectives to surface.
3. *Dialogue Over Monologue:* Meetings, like the best conversations, are two-way streets. Leaders should facilitate balanced participation - encouraging quieter voices while managing dominant ones. This ensures meetings are dynamic discussions rather than boring status reports.

4. *Purpose-Driven Engagement:* Every meeting must have a clear purpose, much like meaningful conversations have a reason behind them. When people understand the "why" behind a meeting, they engage more authentically, knowing their contributions matter.
5. *Building Long-Term Trust:* The same way repeated meaningful conversations build lasting relationships, consistent, well-run meetings strengthen professional relationships. Over time, these interactions foster trust, alignment, and a sense of belonging among team members.
6. *Keep them short.* Crazy one-hour meetings were the norm. Like what did we even talk about?

And finally, coordinating meetings across time zones sounds simple in theory - but in practice, it's a leadership challenge that requires intentionality.

In a world of remote work, where teams are distributed across continents, thoughtful scheduling isn't just logistics - it's a signal of respect. It shows you understand that time zones are more than numbers on a clock; they reflect the realities of people's lives and routines. I know this from experience. Operating out of California, I collaborate with partners across Europe, the Middle East, Asia, and Africa - often around the clock. In today's global workforce, aligning schedules isn't just about convenience; it's about fostering engagement, trust, and inclusivity. Leaders who excel in global collaboration understand that meetings are not just events - they are investments in relationships.

It's a good practice to acknowledge the effort people make to join meetings - like saying, 'Good morning, Jan. Thanks for calling in - it's 5 a.m. for you in Berlin.'

Small gestures like this show your team that you see them and appreciate their commitment. However, it's even better to avoid scheduling meetings at odd hours altogether. Thoughtful scheduling isn't just polite - it builds trust and signals that you respect your team's time and well-being. In a globally distributed workforce, success lies in fostering alignment without burning people out. The best leaders don't just run meetings - they run them with empathy.

Anyways, MQ blends strategic thinking with emotional awareness, creating an environment where ideas flourish and decisions get made. Think of it as a hybrid of Emotional Intelligence (EQ) and Operational Efficiency. Leaders with high MQ know how to align their team's energy, create trust, and drive meaningful outcomes from every conversation.

This goes beyond the superficial advice of "set agendas" or "take notes." MQ is about understanding the psychology of meetings, managing group dynamics, and orchestrating discussions to achieve the desired outcomes. It's about knowing who to invite, how to structure the conversation, and when to pivot. Leaders with MQ can read the room - whether virtual or in-person - and adjust their strategy on the fly.

Master the Art of High-Quality Meetings

1. Objective: Why Are We Here?

Every meeting needs a reason for being. Leaders with high MQ know how to distill the purpose of a meeting into a single, actionable statement. Whether it's aligning on a project, brainstorming new ideas, or reviewing progress, the meeting's objective must be crystal clear - a clear objective!

- *Example:* Instead of calling a generic "weekly sync," frame the meeting as "Aligning on Deliverables for Q4 Marketing Launch."
- Start meetings with a quick review of the objective - this ensures everyone is aligned from the beginning.

2. Making Every Voice Count

Effective meetings create space for every participant to contribute meaningfully. This is particularly important in hybrid environments, where remote attendees can easily feel left out. Leaders with high MQ design interactions to keep participants engaged throughout the meeting.

- *Actionable Tip:* Use real-time polls or breakout rooms to involve participants actively.
- *Insight:* The more engaged participants feel, the more likely they are to leave the meeting with a sense of accomplishment and connection.
- *Relevant:* It is your job to make sure every invitee brings value and has a meaningful role. Ask yourself - and clearly communicate to each participant - why they are invited and what you expect from them. If you don't have time to define this, it may be a sign the meeting shouldn't happen at all.
- *Reflect and distribute:* Critical decisions don't end when the meeting wraps - they need space to breathe. Taking time for reflection allows quieter participants to process

the discussion and contribute insights they might not have shared in the moment. Encourage a break or a follow-up session to revisit key points with fresh eyes. This not only ensures better outcomes but also promotes inclusion, giving every voice a chance to shape the final decision. And remember - decisions are only as good as their execution. If they don't make it beyond the meeting room to those responsible for implementation, they're worthless. You'd be surprised how often decisions die on the table simply because they're not communicated effectively.

3. Time Management: The Power of Punctuality

In meetings, how you show up reflects how you lead. Being punctual isn't just a courtesy - it's a way of communicating respect. Too often, leaders fall into the trap of treating meetings as obligations, arriving late and sending the wrong message to those waiting.

By practicing punctuality, leaders signal that they value others' time and contributions. Small actions like showing up on time compound into trust - and trust is the foundation of effective meetings. Leaders who cultivate this habit don't just run smoother meetings; they build stronger relationships.

We are what we practice. If you consistently respect others' time in meetings, you build a culture of accountability and mutual respect. These small gestures reflect the core principles of Meeting Intelligence: clear communication, purposeful interaction, and trust-building. Time is the one resource we never get back, and poorly managed meetings are the biggest culprits in draining it. Meetings should start and end on time, with clear time-boxing for each agenda item.

- Example: A 45-minute meeting creates buffer time between back-to-back meetings, allowing participants to stay fresh and engaged.

- Assign someone to act as a timekeeper, gently reminding the group to stay on track.

Startup founders, for example, don't have time to waste - every minute counts. In the excellent book "The Hard Thing About Hard Things", Ben Horowitz mentions that at a16z investment fund, the partners are fined $10 for every minute they're late to a founder meeting.

Here's a real-life example, a quote that many of us can relate to:

"Every so often when I book a meeting with someone (a call, not in person) they will just.... not show up. This happened to me yesterday after confirming a mutually agreeable time (that they suggested) and sending the meeting request with call-in details and confirming the time by email. In these situations, what are your next steps? Do you email them to try to find another time? Wait for them to email you with an explanation/apology? Consider them too flaky to meet with and give up on pursuing a meeting with them? Some other things?"

What would your advice be in this situation?

4. Follow-Through: Turning Talk into Action

A meeting without follow-up is like planting a garden and never watering it. Leaders with high MQ document decisions and assign clear next steps to ensure that the time spent in meetings translates into action.

- *Actionable Tip:* Use a **post-meeting recap** to capture key takeaways and assign ownership for action items.
- *Insight:* Meetings are only as valuable as the follow-up actions they generate.

Finally, I think to maintain a healthy organization, companies should occasionally wipe the slate clean by deleting all recurring meetings.

This strategy creates a necessary back pressure, forcing teams to reassess the value and purpose of each meeting. If a meeting can't be justified on its merits, it doesn't come back. The result? Fewer unnecessary meetings and more focus on meaningful work.

As a leader, you must consistently drive effective communication. Meetings must be deliberate and intentional – your organizational rhythm should value purpose over habit and effectiveness over efficiency.

Chris Fussell

Why MQ Matters in the Future of Work

Research shows that companies with strong meeting cultures have lower turnover rates and higher employee engagement. Leaders who develop MQ will position their organizations for success in the new world of work.

Practical Tools to Develop MQ in Your Organization

1. *Agenda Templates:* Create structured agendas that align with the meeting's purpose.

2. *Pre-cap:* share a pre-cap - it sets the tone for a meeting by ensuring alignment before participants even walk in (or log on). It provides clarity around objectives, introduces attendees who may not know each other, and includes any prep work to ensure meaningful contributions. A pre-cap also establishes expectations - like whether cameras should be on and who's responsible for notetaking. This proactive approach primes everyone for engagement and keeps meetings focused, efficient, and intentional. It's a small investment that yields big returns in productivity and trust.

3. *Feedback Loops:* Gathering feedback after key meetings is essential for continuous improvement. Every meeting should end with a quick 'Was this meeting worth your time? Yes or No.' The results should go directly to the CFO as a meeting score. If more than 12% of meetings are deemed unproductive, that's a red flag - one that demands action. Respectfully, it signals a deeper issue with how time and resources are being managed.

4. *Technology Tools:* Use technology platforms to manage meeting flow and capture real-time insights.

5. *Role Rotation:* Rotate roles such as facilitator, timekeeper, and note-taker to foster engagement. AI-generated notes are useful, but a human touch is essential. When a person

takes notes, they become more concise, actionable, and memorable. The act of writing also sharpens focus and retention. And let's be honest - most AI-generated transcripts are rarely reviewed thoroughly. Combining AI with human insight ensures meeting takeaways are meaningful and actionable. Assigning roles in meetings keeps things organized and makes sure everyone shares the load. When roles like note-taker, timekeeper, or facilitator are clear, meetings run smoother, and no one person is always "stuck" doing the same task. It's funny how it often ends up being the same person taking notes - usually because they're "just so good at it." But constantly sticking to one person with this role can lead to burnout and frustration. By mixing it up, everyone gets a chance to contribute in different ways, keeping things fair and helping the whole team stay engaged.

6. *Educating and training.* Expecting people to run meetings without guidance is like handing someone a car without a driver's license. It never made sense to me how an (newly hired) employee can jump straight into hosting meetings without proper training or alignment with the company's values. Meeting culture isn't just about logistics - it's a reflection of your company's broader culture. When done right, meetings shape how people collaborate, communicate, and build trust. If you want to foster a high-performance culture, it starts with teaching people how to run meetings that matter. Imagine everyone in your organization earning a black belt in meetings - how powerful would that be? With every team member mastering the art of effective meetings, the results would

be game-changing: fewer wasted hours, sharper focus, and actionable outcomes. Now that's a skill worth investing in.

Chapter 2: The Future of Work and Meeting Expectations

While meetings have always been a staple of corporate life, their role in the hybrid world has become even more critical. As companies adapt to new ways of working, Meeting Intelligence (MQ) becomes the crucial skill that determines whether meetings drive success or stifle productivity.

The Hybrid Revolution: More Flexibility, Higher Expectations

We've entered an era where flexibility is not a perk; it's a demand. A 2023 study by McKinsey found that more than 70% of employees prefer hybrid work models, combining the best of remote and in-office environments. They want freedom, not (just) flexibility.

But this shift has also come with new challenges. Hybrid workforces face increased complexity, as teams are spread across geographies, time zones, and schedules. Meetings are often the only real-time touchpoint where all these pieces come together. So, what does this mean for leaders? It means that meetings must evolve, or they risk becoming irrelevant and frustrating to employees. The days of in-person meetings where body language and informal chats could fill in the gaps are gone. Today, meeting expectations are higher than ever, and the margin for error is slim.

Employees want meetings that are:

- *Purpose-driven:* Clear objectives and outcomes must be defined upfront.
- *Inclusive:* Everyone, whether remote or in-office, should feel heard and involved.
- *Efficient:* Time is more valuable than ever. Meetings should be short, structured, and to the point.
- *Relevant:* for their job, projects, skills and future career plans.

The Costs of Poor Meetings in the Hybrid World

In the traditional office setting, a poorly run meeting could lead to an eyeroll or two. In the hybrid world, however, the stakes are much higher.

Inefficient meetings have a ripple effect across organizations, leading to lost productivity, employee burnout, and even higher turnover. Research from Stanford University found that poorly managed hybrid meetings are one of the top reasons employees feel disconnected and disengaged in their roles!

People who enjoy meetings should not be in charge of anything.

Thomas Sowell

The Hybrid Disconnect

The challenges of hybrid work are clear. Remote employees often feel like second-class citizens during meetings. While in-office participants can easily jump in with spontaneous comments or enjoy side conversations, remote workers are left waiting for their turn to speak. This imbalance not only damages team cohesion, but it also discourages participation from remote workers.

The Productivity Drain

According to MIT, companies lose an average of $37 billion annually due to unnecessary meetings. This problem is exacerbated in the hybrid world, where the temptation to "over-communicate" leads to even more time wasted. Managers, unsure how to maintain connection and alignment with their dispersed teams, often default to scheduling more meetings - leading to Zoom fatigue, burnout, and reduced engagement. A Microsoft found that 73% of employees report experiencing burnout from the constant stream of virtual meetings.

Rethinking Meeting Expectations

To meet the needs of the modern workforce, companies must rethink their meeting practices and culture, requiring leaders to adopt new strategies that balance the needs of both remote and in-office workers.

1. Shift to Asynchronous Communication

Not every discussion needs to happen in real-time. In fact, asynchronous communication - where team members share updates and collaborate across different times - has become a key solution for hybrid teams. This also allows employees to engage with the material at their own pace, rather than sitting through long, unfocused calls.

Asynchronous meetings allow for greater flexibility and give people more time to reflect on their contributions. This leads to better decision-making and less meeting fatigue.

Reid Hoffman

2. Virtual-First Agenda

In hybrid meetings, the focus must shift to a virtual-first agenda. This means designing the meeting experience with remote participants as the priority. If your meeting is hybrid, treat the virtual experience as the main platform, and ensure remote attendees have equal opportunity to participate.

Example: A company adopted a "remote-first" mindset, where even in-office participants dial into the meeting virtually to ensure everyone has an equal seat at the table, literally.

As a board member of several international companies, I'm often the only one joining remotely. In some meetings, I've experienced the frustration of being overlooked - whether it's not being able to indicate I have a question, the chat not being monitored, or simply being forgotten. Hybrid meetings require intentional design to ensure every participant, regardless of location, can engage meaningfully. Without clear signals and structure, remote members risk being sidelined.

Hybrid meetings require intentional human and technological design and clear expectations from the start. Without structure, in-person side chats can isolate remote participants, and distractions like virtual attendees stepping away mid-meeting can derail the flow. Leaders who master this balance will unlock the real power of hybrid collaboration.

3. Shorter, More Frequent Check-ins

The traditional hour-long meeting is outdated in the hybrid world. Instead, shorter, more frequent 10- 15-minute check-ins have proven to be more effective. These quick stand-ups help maintain alignment without overwhelming employees' schedules.

4. Meeting-Free Days

Research from Harvard Business School shows that implementing meeting-free days leads to a boost in productivity and employee well-being. By designating specific days for deep work, companies create space for employees to focus on their core responsibilities without constant interruptions.

Be careful - banning meetings on certain days can backfire, cramming them into others and defeating the purpose. Some companies, like Shopify, have taken a different approach, showing employees the real cost of their meetings in lost productivity. This subtle nudge makes people more deliberate about scheduling, reinforcing that time is a precious resource. The goal isn't just fewer meetings - it's smarter ones that add value. Leaders who master this approach will unlock better focus, creativity, and engagement across their teams.

What if booking internal meetings costs company "tokens"? Suddenly, meetings wouldn't just fill calendars - they'd hit wallets. Tracking token spend could reveal who's inflating the organization with unnecessary meetings. This system forces people to think twice - only the essential meetings survive. After all, if time is money, we should spend both wisely.

Has anyone ever said, 'I wish I could go to more meetings today'?

Matt Mullenweg

Why Meeting Intelligence is Key to the Future of Work

As the workplace continues to evolve, so must our approach to meetings. The companies that will thrive in the future are those that embrace change and adopt Meeting Intelligence as a core skill.

MQ allows leaders to:

- Run meetings that matter, focusing on clarity, engagement, and action.
- Reduce meeting fatigue, by balancing real-time and asynchronous collaboration.
- Foster inclusion, ensuring that all voices - remote and in-office—are heard equally.

The hybrid world presents a unique opportunity for companies to rethink their meeting culture and build a more efficient, inclusive workplace. Leaders who develop their MQ will not only survive in the new world of work - they'll be the ones shaping it.

Practical Takeaways for Leaders

1. *Adopt a Virtual-First Mindset:* Design meetings with remote participants as the priority.
2. *Shorten Your Meetings:* Aim for 15–20-minute stand-ups to keep communication crisp and focused.

3. *Embrace Asynchronous Collaboration:* Use tools like Slack and Loom to cut down on unnecessary meetings.

4. *Implement Meeting-Free Days:* Designate one day a week for deep work to boost productivity.

The future of work is hybrid, and Meeting Intelligence is the key to unlocking success in this new era. Leaders who master these strategies will build high-performing, resilient teams that thrive in the face of change.

> *Meetings should have as few people as possible, but all the right people.*
>
> **Charles W. Scharf**

Next, we'll dive into how to foster engagement in meetings, ensuring that every participant, whether remote or in-office, feels heard and valued.

Chapter 3: Fostering Engagement - Unlocking the Power of Participation

The Neuroscience of Engagement: Why Participation Is the Key to Meeting Success

Engagement is not just a buzzword; it's a fundamental ingredient for effective collaboration. According to a study by MIT Sloan, participants in highly engaging meetings are 33% more likely to retain information and 40% more likely to feel motivated to act.

But engagement doesn't happen by accident - it must be deliberately cultivated.

For a short while, I wore a brain scanner from Emotiv during meetings - it looks like a simple headset, but it tracks attention, stress, and mental focus. Now, I know when I'm bored or distracted, but seeing the data was eye-opening. It was fascinating to learn just how often I mentally checked out, how long it took to refocus after sneaking a glance at a text, and how stress built up over time. It's one thing to feel it - another to see it quantified in real-time.

The Anatomy of Engagement: What It Looks Like in Practice

Engaged participants aren't just nodding along - they're actively contributing, asking questions, and collaborating. Here are the hallmarks of an engaging meeting:

1. *Interactive Dialogue:* Discussions flow in multiple directions, not just from leader to team.
2. *Diverse Input:* Different perspectives are invited and encouraged.
3. *Real-Time Problem Solving:* Participants feel empowered to solve challenges during the meeting.
4. *Energy and Momentum:* The pace keeps participants mentally present and focused.

Want to know if people are truly engaged in your meeting? Don't rely on gut instinct - track the signs. Research shows that body language, eye movement, and speech patterns are reliable indicators of focus. Engagement also drops sharply after the 30-minute mark, with studies suggesting productivity can fall by up to 40% as meetings drag on.

The trick isn't just monitoring participation - it's structuring meetings to be worth their attention. Short, purpose-driven calls and active involvement keep participants engaged and aligned. Keep virtual meetings engaging by using interactive tools like polls and breakout rooms, incorporating visual aids, and encouraging active participation.

Vary presentation styles, manage time effectively, and foster connection through activities like icebreakers and Q&A sessions. Encourage participants to turn on video and use chat for real-time interaction. Facilitate discussions actively, offering opportunities for input and ending with reflections. Tailor your approach to participant preferences, ensuring meetings stay dynamic and meaningful. This sounds so easy, but it is really not. Are you great at engaging with people?

Think about networking events, talks, or meetings - how do people respond to you? If you're not seeing lively, engaged eyes during calls or conversations, it's time to level up. Engagement isn't just about speaking - it's about connecting, sparking curiosity, and leaving people energized. If you're not getting that kind of response, refine your approach and sharpen your communication skills. Great leaders inspire interaction and enthusiasm - are you?

Personally, I like to take 2-5 minutes between meetings to reset. It helps me shake off the energy from the previous call and recenter my mind. I focus on positive thoughts to ensure I don't carry over any lingering negativity into the next conversation. Often you have to jump from one situation to another with little to no time in between. Mastering mental clarity and emotional control is essential to stay sharp and lead effectively - this is the key to maintaining 'mental sobriety' throughout the day.

One of my professors at Harvard taught me a simple but powerful technique - look at something that makes you happy right before a meeting. It could be a picture of your pet, child, partner, or even a flower - whatever lifts your spirits. Even a screen saver will do.

This small habit helps shift your mindset, allowing you to enter meetings in a more positive, friendly frame of mind. It's a subtle trick, but it can make all the difference in how you show up

Meetings should be like salt – a spice sprinkled carefully to enhance a dish, not poured recklessly over every forkful. Too much salt destroys a dish. Too many meetings destroy morale and motivation.

Jason Fried

Techniques to Drive Engagement Before, During, and After Meetings

1. *Pre-Meeting Engagement: Setting the Stage for Participation*

Engagement starts before the meeting even begins. Leaders can send pre-reading materials, agenda previews, or even short surveys to get participants thinking about the topic ahead of time.

- Example: Before a strategy session, send participants three thought-provoking questions and ask them to come prepared with ideas. This primes them to engage meaningfully from the start.
- Use a tool like Loom to record a quick video introduction - this personal touch boosts interest.

2. *Facilitate Dynamic Conversations During Meetings*

Incorporate structured activities to prevent one-way conversations. Interactive exercises like brainstorming sessions, role-playing, or live polling ensure everyone participates.

3. Post-Meeting Engagement: Reinforcing Participation

High MQ leaders **follow up effectively** to keep the momentum going. After the meeting, send participants a **summary of action items**, along with a brief feedback survey. This not only reinforces key points but also encourages continuous improvement.

And here are some strategies for politely managing dominating voices in meetings and encouraging balanced participation:

1. Set Ground Rules Up Front

- At the start, introduce a structure like time limits for speaking.
- Example: *"To keep things efficient, let's aim to limit responses to one minute each."*
- This makes the structure the guide, not you.

2. Use Gentle Interruption Techniques

- Politely step in with phrases like:
    - *"That's an important point, let's hear from others too."*
    - *"Thanks for sharing - now let's get another perspective on this."*
    - *"I'd love to circle back to this, but let's park it for now to stay on track."*

3. Ask Direct Questions to Others

- Draw quieter participants in with specific questions:

- "Sarah, what are your thoughts on this?"
- "Let's hear from someone who hasn't spoken yet - John?"

4. Use a 'Round-Robin' Format

- Go around the room to ensure everyone gets a chance to speak.
- Example: *"Let's take two minutes each to share thoughts before opening it up."*

5. Introduce the 'Traffic Light' Approach

- Use green, yellow, and red cards (or verbal cues) to signal when discussion is on track, veering off-topic, or needs to pause.
- Example: *"We're getting into the weeds - let's bring it back to the agenda."*

6. Appoint a Facilitator or Timekeeper

- Assign someone to manage speaking time and redirect conversations as needed.
- Example: *"As the timekeeper, I'll remind us to move on if we're running long."*

7. Follow Up One-on-One

- If someone repeatedly dominates, have a private conversation.
- Example: *"I appreciate your input, but let's ensure everyone has space to contribute."*

Framework for Building Engagement into Every Meeting

Use this engagement framework to ensure every meeting is a platform for active participation:

1. *Prepare and Prime:* Share meeting objectives and key questions in advance.
2. *Design for Interaction:* Use tools like polls, breakout rooms, and whiteboards to keep discussions dynamic.
3. *Rotate Roles:* Assign rotating facilitators to foster shared ownership and fresh perspectives.
4. *Capture and Act:* Send out post-meeting recaps with clear next steps.

The ROI of Engagement: Why It Matters for Business Success

Organizations with high levels of meeting engagement report:

- 35% higher employee satisfaction (Source: Stanford University)
- 22% lower turnover rates (Source: MIT Sloan)
- 15% faster decision-making (Source: INSEAD)

Engagement is not just about making meetings more enjoyable - it's about driving business outcomes. Leaders who master this skill will not only build stronger teams but also position their organizations for success in the future of work.

Chapter 4: Purpose-Driven Meetings - Avoiding Timewasters

The Cost of Unnecessary Meetings

Meetings that lack purpose drain time, life quality, energy, and resources. Studies by Harvard Business Review reveal that unproductive meetings cost U.S. companies an estimated $37 billion annually.

Beyond the monetary loss, poorly run meetings frustrate employees, erode trust, and contribute to burnout.

Burnout isn't a personal issue solved by yoga or mindfulness - it's a systemic problem organization must address head-on.

The real solution lies in building prevention-focused strategies, not perks. Leaders need to measure burnout, reshape meeting cultures, and foster resilience at the organizational level. As Jennifer Moss highlights in *The Burnout Epidemic*, it's time for companies to take the lead and break the chronic stress cycle. Meetings should either solve a problem, align the team, or advance a project - if not, they should be eliminated or replaced with an asynchronous update. We need to kill many more meetings before the meetings!

I hit severe burnout, though the signs had been there long before. The first ambulance ride came in 2001, and by 2012, I realized the anxiety and exhaustion had taken their toll. I was juggling a demanding career, two young kids, extensive travel, and the role of breadwinner. I lost my hair, shed an unhealthy amount of weight, and felt completely drained of joy and purpose. It took years to recover, but I learned to say no - cutting out non-essential work, meetings, and dead-end projects. My 'BS filter' became sharper than ever. It felt incredible that I've been able to dedicate my life to freeing up time for millions through our AI tool, Happioh. Becoming the best AI tool of 2024 wasn't just a professional achievement - it was a deeply personal milestone for me. It's fulfilling to see how something born from my own experience with burnout is now helping others reclaim their time and energy at scale.

My Meeting Policy: If there's no clear objective, I cancel. If the purpose of my invitation isn't obvious, I decline. To be honest, I prefer online meetings over in-person ones. I'm not a fan of video messages or voicemail either - I find texts, video calls, and emails much more effective. If more than seven people are attending and there's no designated note-taker, I skip. I don't do "catch-up coffee" meetings.

No ambiguity. No wasted time. Full stop.

The Anatomy of a Purpose-Driven Meeting

A purpose-driven meeting achieves three core goals:

1. *Clear Objectives:* The desired outcome is defined upfront.

2. *Relevant Participants:* Only those who are essential to the discussion are invited.

3. *Actionable Outcomes:* Every participant leaves knowing what's next.

Meetings that meet these criteria become catalysts for progress, while those that don't become timewasters.

The RACI Framework: Who Needs to Be in the Room?

One common mistake in meetings is over-inviting participants, leading to bloated conversations. Leaders with high MQ use the RACI Framework (Responsible, Accountable, Consulted, Informed) to determine who should attend:

- *Responsible:* The person(s) doing the work.
- *Accountable:* The decision-maker.
- *Consulted:* Those who provide input.
- *Informed:* Those who need to know the outcome.

If someone falls under the "Informed" category, consider sending them a meeting summary rather than having them attend the entire session.

How to Design a Purpose-Driven Meeting

1. *Start with a Clear Goal / Objective:* Before sending out an invite, define the **desired outcome** of the meeting. **Example:** Instead of "Weekly Team Sync," use "Align on Q4 Launch Plan Deliverables." This shift makes the meeting's focus clear and actionable.

2. *Create a Detailed Agenda:* A strong agenda serves as a meeting roadmap. It keeps discussions focused and ensures all topics are covered within the allotted time. Make sure everyone knows what their part of the agenda is. Share the agenda 24 hours in advance so participants can come prepared.

3. *Stick to Time Limits*: Meetings that run over time signal poor planning. Use timeboxing techniques - assign specific time limits to each agenda item to keep things on track.

4. *Track:* who completes the prep work before meetings. If someone shows up unprepared, consider rescheduling the call. Meetings are most effective when all participants are ready to engage - unprepared attendees waste time and derail progress. **Example:** Allot 10 minutes for status updates and 10 minutes for brainstorming solutions.

5. *End with Action Items:* Every meeting should conclude with a summary of **decisions made** and **next steps**. Assign clear ownership to ensure follow-through.

I don't do meetings.

Karl Lagerfeld

Case Study: Shopify's Purpose-Driven Meeting Culture

Shopify underwent a cultural shift in 2022 by eliminating recurring meetings and introducing strict guidelines on meeting participation. They saw a 30% reduction in meeting hours and reported higher employee morale. This shift allowed teams to focus on deep work and reserve meetings for high-priority discussions only.

Checklist: How to Make Every Meeting Purposeful

- *Define the Goal:* Why are we meeting? What decision or outcome do we want?
- *Invite the Right People:* Use the **RACI framework** to determine participants.

- *Create and Share an Agenda:* Send it in advance so attendees can prepare.

- *Use Timeboxing:* Assign time limits to each agenda item.

- *End with Action Items:* Document decisions and assign next steps.

The ROI of Purpose-Driven Meetings

Organizations that adopt purpose-driven meeting practices report:

- *15% faster project completion times.*

- *30% higher employee satisfaction.*

- *20% fewer meeting hours per month.*

Purposeful meetings not only save time but also build trust and momentum. When every meeting has a clear goal and actionable outcomes, teams stay aligned, motivated, and productive.

"Some days, I both love and hate project meetings - right now, I'm leaning more toward hate. Every week, I dedicate a full day to these meetings. The frustrating part? Most of what's discussed doesn't even involve me. But the real kicker is that if I skip, I miss critical updates that directly affect my work, forcing me to scramble when things go sideways. If I'm not in the room to raise concerns, decisions are made that can completely derail my plans. And it works the other way too - they have no idea what my job entails, so they don't know what they should be asking me." anonymous worker in a construction company.

Chapter 5: The Role of Leadership in Shaping Meeting Culture

Why Leadership Sets the Tone for Meeting Culture

Meeting culture starts at the top. Leaders play a pivotal role in defining whether meetings become a platform for innovation and alignment or a frustrating time drain. A leader's attitude toward meetings sets the standard for the entire organization.

If leaders show up unprepared, distracted, or late, that behavior will trickle down to the rest of the team. Conversely, when leaders model engagement, punctuality, and focus, they create a culture where meetings are taken seriously and add value.

The Ripple Effect of Poor Leadership in Meetings

In *The Hard Thing About Hard Things*, Ben Horowitz highlights the importance of clear communication and well-structured meetings.

One key insight is that the purpose and expectations of meetings should be explicit - when meetings lack structure, they tend to waste time and create misalignment. Horowitz also emphasizes that meetings, especially one-on-ones, are critical tools for managers to understand challenges within the organization and build trust. Without regular, intentional communication through meetings, leaders risk becoming disconnected from their teams and missing crucial insights about the health of the organization. He critiques leaders who let meetings become barriers instead of tools, reinforcing that intentional meeting culture is essential for organizational success. His insights align well with the idea that effective meetings aren't just logistical - they're fundamental to leadership, team cohesion, and strategic clarity.

Leaders need to go beyond simply scheduling meetings - they must design them to build trust, ensure engagement, and drive actionable outcomes. This mindset shifts meetings from being a necessary evil to becoming a core leadership tool. Leaders must carefully balance between productive communication and minimizing unnecessary meetings to avoid draining their teams' focus and energy.

Poorly run meetings can truly demoralize teams, waste resources, and foster a culture of disengagement. Employees who feel their time is wasted are more likely to:

- *Lose motivation* to actively participate in future meetings.
- *Withdraw from collaborative efforts,* leading to communication breakdowns.
- *Experience burnout,* contributing to higher turnover rates.

In contrast, leaders who take ownership of meetings build trust, foster engagement, and drive better outcomes. With the sheer volume of meetings growing, it's critical to rethink how time is spent and make intentional changes to improve productivity.

Two immediate adjustments can create quick wins:

1. *Eliminate unnecessary recurring meetings.* Many meetings exist out of habit rather than necessity. Cutting redundant ones clears space for more meaningful work.

2. *Adopt a structured meeting framework.* One example worth exploring is **Level 10 (L10)** meetings, a framework designed to streamline discussions and keep teams on track.

Here's what makes the L10 framework effective:

- *Consistent structure:* Every meeting follows the same agenda, ensuring focus and momentum.

- *Inclusive participation:* All team members have the opportunity to contribute, fostering collaboration.

- *Solution-focused:* Conversations revolve around solving problems and achieving goals, not just sharing updates.

- *Built-in accountability:* Regular touchpoints help track performance and resolve issues quickly.

Using even a modified version of this approach can help teams stay aligned, concentrate on high-priority work, and operate more efficiently. For those facing packed schedules - like school administrators - this structure offers a smart way to reduce meeting fatigue while improving outcomes. And no, meetings don't need to last 90 minutes to be effective

I hate meetings that are a giant waste of time for everyone involved. Anytime we have a department meeting we spend half the time playing some sort of stupid "team building" game.

Anonymous worker in a tech company.

Recently a senior executive called me after I suggested they join a call with a potential partner in Europe. Shortly after, she texted me saying, "I left that meeting after 10 minutes, the energy in that virtual room was horrible."

We debriefed, and I followed up with the partner to let them know we'd be stepping away from the project. Bad meetings and toxic behavior should never be tolerated, they need to be called out and addressed. Don't hesitate to walk out of "rooms" that don't align with your values or standards. Your team is watching the behavior you choose to allow

How Leaders Can Model Meeting Excellence

1. *Be Punctual and Prepared:* Leaders must lead by example by arriving on time and reviewing the agenda beforehand. This demonstrates respect for participants' time and sets the tone for a focused discussion.

2. *Foster Psychological Safety:* Create a space where participants feel comfortable sharing ideas without fear of judgement. Leaders with high MQ actively solicit feedback and encourage diverse perspectives. **Example:** Use the phrase, "What am I missing?" to invite alternative viewpoints and show openness to feedback.

3. *Engage Actively:* Leaders must stay mentally present throughout the meeting. Avoid distractions (like checking emails) and focus fully on the discussion at hand. Participants mirror the leader's engagement level, so staying involved encourages others to do the same.

4. *Hold Participants Accountable:* Effective leaders track follow-through on meeting action items. They use tools like project management software to monitor progress and ensure accountability.

5. *Include goals & progress:* updates from department leaders, share roadblocks & debate on key questions between attendees, share key questions/solutions so people can execute.

6. *Be bold:* If a meeting isn't achieving its objective, don't be afraid to hit pause. Say, 'Let's stop here and pick this up tomorrow or next week.' There's no need to push through a meeting if it's not working. Sometimes the timing isn't right and forcing it won't get better results. There have been moments where unexpected insights arise when participants are given time to reflect - other times, calling it quits early saves everyone time and energy.

"We often jump into meetings expecting alignment and quick agreements. When that happens, fantastic - everyone's on the same page, and the team can immediately focus on next steps. But when disagreements arise or alignment falls apart, the meeting drags, momentum slips, and before you know it, you're scheduling yet another follow-up meeting. Cue eye rolls all around. I've been there. More than once, I've had to send invites with this message: "This is the follow-up meeting

because the last one ended like Avengers: Infinity War - everyone scattered, no closure, and half the room emotionally wiped out." The solution? Pre-meetings with key stakeholders. Keep them short and targeted. Use them to share your analysis, test the waters, and address concerns before the official kick-off. While this won't guarantee a perfectly smooth meeting, it'll significantly reduce the surprises - and save you from unnecessary sequels."

James Chang

During a discovery workshop with Mastercard, we learned about their approach to meetings, called the "Meeting Burger." This simple yet powerful framework breaks meetings into three distinct phases: before, during, and after - each represented by a layer of a burger.

- *Before the Meeting (Bottom Bun)* - Just like a solid base for a burger, the pre-meeting phase is crucial for setting up success. It's about defining objectives, setting a clear agenda, and ensuring all necessary information is provided ahead of time. This helps everyone come prepared and aligned.
- *During the Meeting (Burger Filling)* - This is where the main action happens, and Mastercard's approach emphasizes three key principles:
    1. *Stick to the schedule and agenda* - Respect everyone's time by staying on track.
    2. *Engage all voices* - As the meeting leader, ensure everyone is heard and involved, creating an inclusive space.

3. *Add energy* - Break up the session with a brief 2–5-minute activity, like a quick icebreaker or energizer, to keep things lively and focused.

- *After the Meeting (Top Bun)* - This phase ties everything together, ensuring action items are clear, follow-ups are scheduled, and any necessary feedback is collected. This wrap-up helps reinforce accountability and closes the loop.

By focusing on these three phases, meeting organizers can create sessions that are clear, productive, and - dare I say - satisfying!

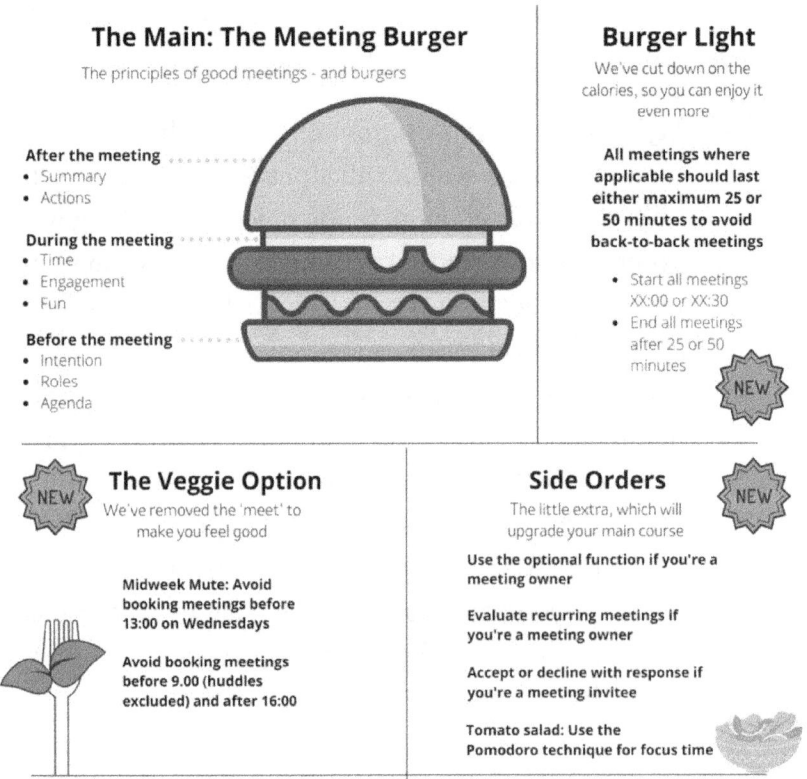

Feedback Loops: Continuous Improvement for Meeting Culture

High MQ leaders understand the importance of **continuous feedback**. They regularly seek input from their teams to identify what's working and what needs improvement in meetings. It is very simple: "Leaders must know what to do and must get people to do what needs to be done."

I recently spoke with the co-chair of two of the largest companies in the world, and they shared something insightful: asking for feedback is tough, especially at the executive level. Even at the top, seeking honest feedback can feel vulnerable and challenging.

Why is feedback so hard to receive? For one, feedback often challenges our sense of self and can bring up insecurities, no matter how experienced we are. We naturally want to focus on our strengths, but constructive feedback, while valuable, can feel personal and uncomfortable.

To be mentally prepared for feedback, it helps to approach it with a growth mindset—seeing feedback not as criticism but as a tool for personal and professional development. Remind yourself that every insight, even if it's tough to hear, is an opportunity to grow stronger in your role. And practice gratitude for feedback, knowing it's ultimately a gift that helps you reach your full potential. The more open and curious we are, the easier it becomes to accept feedback and use it to fuel improvement.

- After key meetings, send a quick survey asking participants: *How effective was this meeting? What could we improve next time? Was it worth your time?*

Mastering the Art of Feedback

- *Stay positive (yes, really!):* Let's be honest, most of us thrive on a little encouragement. But we live in a world that loves pointing out flaws. Sure, take the critiques seriously, but don't forget to high-five yourself for the wins, too!
- *Be specific (no mystery feedback)* The clearer the feedback, the easier it is to use. Ask for specifics! "Work on this" is fine, but "Here's what to try next time" is where the magic happens.
- *Keep it real (and doable)* Feedback is only helpful if it's something you can act on. Look for advice you can put to use without a total overhaul.
- *Check their motives:* Before you dive into the feedback, consider the source. Are they looking out for you, or maybe (just maybe) hoping to feel a bit better about themselves? Feedback with good intentions always lands better.
- *Listen first, defend late:* Hear them out before jumping in with your side. What are they saying? Keep an open mind - there might be some gold in there.
- *Ignore what doesn't click (within reason):* Not every piece of feedback will feel useful, and that's okay. But if you're hearing the same thing from multiple people, it might be worth a second look.

- *Ask for what you need:* Sometimes we need help in specific areas, but people can't read minds. Don't be shy—ask for feedback that'll make a difference for you.

Feedback doesn't have to be a drag. With a little humor and some self-awareness, you'll be a feedback pro in no time!

Consider recording some of your meetings to analyze not only how you deliver your message but also how your team responds. Watching the recording afterward allows you to observe their reactions to your words, tone, and delivery, giving you valuable insight into what resonates and what might need adjusting. This simple practice can reveal so much about the dynamics of your communication and help you improve how you connect with your team.

The Strategic Role of Meetings in Leadership Development

Meetings offer more than just a venue for decision-making - they are also **training grounds for future leaders**. High MQ leaders use meetings to mentor and coach their teams, developing the next generation of leadership talent.

- Remember to rotate facilitation responsibilities among team members to give emerging leaders hands-on experience in running meetings.

Checklist: How Leaders Can Shape a Positive Meeting Culture

- *Model Good Behavior:* Be punctual, prepared, and engaged in every meeting.

- *Foster Accountability:* Track action items and follow up on commitments.
- *Solicit Feedback:* Use post-meeting surveys to identify areas for improvement.
- *Leverage Data:* Use meeting analytics to monitor performance and optimize practices.
- *Develop Future Leaders:* Rotate meeting roles to build leadership skills across the team.

Establish clear consequences for poor meeting behavior, including sanctions if necessary. Meetings reflect the company's culture, and everyone must align with those standards. If someone consistently fails to meet expectations, it may be time to part ways. A productive meeting culture is non-negotiable - those who can't adapt risk undermining the efficiency and spirit of the organization.

> *Due to the strict salary hierarchy at my current employer, I know exactly how much each head of department earns. I even use an app that calculates how much money is wasted during their weekly meetings. In contrast, my own weekly meetings with my team are far more productive - we reach decisions every time. Our head of department often confides in us that those leadership meetings are nothing more than highly paid people complaining for up to eight hours straight.*

Anonymous worker in a design company.

The ROI of Leadership in Meeting Culture

Organizations with leaders who prioritize meeting excellence report:

- *30% higher employee engagement*
- *22% faster decision-making*
- *15% lower turnover rates*

Leaders who master MQ create a culture where meetings become strategic assets - fostering collaboration, trust, and innovation. These leaders position their organizations for long-term success in the future of work.

About a year ago, we held a workshop at one of the largest organizations in Germany, where a manager shared an eye-opening insight: she had never experienced a meeting that actually ended in a decision. This speaks to the core issue with meetings for many people - they have no interest in cutting down on them, because meetings *are* their work. It's a form of pseudo-productivity, filling time without driving results.

Personally, if I were to consider a role in any organization, I wouldn't accept it unless they could show me, they have systems in place to protect against low-quality meetings.

Chapter 6: Time Management in Meetings - Mastering the Clock

The Cost of Poor Time Management

Few things frustrate employees more than meetings that run over time or discussions that feel endless. According to research from Stanford University, organizations waste more than 10 hours per week per employee due to poorly managed meetings. Leaders with high Meeting Intelligence (MQ) understand that time is a non-renewable resource, and they treat it with the care it deserves. Managing time effectively within meetings not only respects participants but also improves engagement and decision-making.

Elon Musk (Tesla, SpaceX): Musk advises employees to skip meetings where they aren't adding value and to walk out if the meeting isn't clear to them why they are invited. He believes this direct approach improves productivity and frees up time for essential work.

Why Timeboxing is a Game-Changer for Meetings

Timeboxing involves assigning a specific time limit to each segment of the meeting. This technique prevents conversations from dragging on and ensures that every agenda item receives attention. Leaders who use timeboxing:

- *Increase focus* by creating a sense of urgency.

- *Avoid off-topic discussions* that derail the meeting.

- *Foster accountability* by signaling that each participant's time is valuable.

Example: Instead of letting updates consume half the meeting, allocate 10 minutes for reports, 15 minutes for problem-solving, and 5 minutes for action items.

How to Run Efficient Meetings Using Time Management Principles

1. Set a Hard Start and End Time

Meetings should start and end on time, regardless of whether all participants are present. Waiting for latecomers sends the message that punctuality is optional, creating a culture of lateness.

- Use a countdown clock visible to participants to reinforce the time limit.

To keep meetings sharp and prevent them from dragging on, consider introducing a few focused (fun) rules.

Plank meetings, for instance, are a creative way to boost efficiency. Everyone holds a plank while running through updates, keeping discussions tight and energy high. With the time limit naturally built in, people cut to the chase, and by the end, you've covered the essentials and even had a quick workout. For a simpler approach, try "no drinks, no bathroom" meetings. If no one's settling in with a coffee or eyeing an exit, the agenda stays on track. And standing meetings? A tried-and-true tactic: by removing chairs, people stay engaged, direct, and brief. These strategies don't just keep meetings short - they ensure the time spent is high-value and productive. Consider to set a **"No Recap" Rule** - If people miss the start, they catch up on their own. This eliminates that all-too-common recap time for latecomers and encourages punctuality.

2. Use a Consent Agenda

A **consent agenda** consolidates routine items that don't require discussion into a single vote. This frees up meeting time for more important conversations.

- *Example:* At a weekly leadership meeting, a consent agenda might include approval of last week's minutes and routine budget updates.

You could also do a "Decision-Only" Policy for Big Meetings - If it's a large group meeting, only bring items that need decisions. Status updates can go in emails or shared docs, but meetings should be reserved for actions that require real-time input.

3. Limit Meeting Length to 15, 25 or 45 Minutes

Research shows that meetings scheduled for odd lengths - like 25 or 40 minutes - tend to be more focused and productive. These shorter time slots create buffer time between meetings and reduce cognitive fatigue. At Google, many internal meetings are scheduled for 25 minutes, leaving employees time to reset before their next task. And don't invite too many people either. More than 7 people are often not successful.

The Two-Pizza Rule by Jeff Bezos: Meetings shouldn't have more attendees than can be fed with two pizzas.

How to Handle Off-Topic Discussions

Even the most well-planned meetings can go off track. High MQ leaders use "parking lots" - a virtual or physical space to capture off-topic ideas that arise during the meeting. These ideas can be revisited later without disrupting the current agenda.

- Keep a running list of parking lot items and address them during a follow-up meeting or via email.

Checklist: Time Management Best Practices for Meetings

1. *Start and End on Time:* Create a culture of punctuality.
2. *Use Timeboxing:* Allocate time limits to each agenda item.
3. *Leverage Technology:* Use timers and analytics tools to track meeting duration.
4. *Capture Off-Topic Ideas:* Use a parking lot to manage tangents.

The ROI of Effective Time Management

Organizations that adopt time management best practices for meetings report:

- *15% shorter meeting durations*
- *20% higher employee satisfaction*
- *25% faster decision-making*

When meetings respect participants' time, employees are more engaged, motivated, and productive. Leaders who master time management build trust within their teams and foster a culture of efficiency.

You could also consider to implement:

- *Silent Start* - Begin with 5 minutes of quiet reading where everyone reviews the agenda, background materials, or key updates. This reduces time spent "catching up" and ensures everyone's on the same page from the start.
- *One-Way Video Rule for Virtual Meetings* - Turn off all cameras except for the speakers. This encourages everyone to focus on listening rather than managing their own video presence and reduces distractions.
- *"Meeting Curfew"* - Set a strict cutoff time after which no new meetings can be scheduled (e.g., no meetings after 3 p.m.). This respects deep work time and gives people more focused hours in the day.
- *"Two Minutes, Then Move"* - Limit each speaker to a maximum of two minutes per turn. This ensures everyone has a voice without dominating the conversation and keeps discussions tight and action-focused.
- *Last 5 Minutes for Reflection* - Reserve the final few minutes for a quick round where attendees share one thing that went well and one area to improve. It's a fast feedback loop that makes each meeting progressively better.
- *"No Slides" Rule* - Skip the slides entirely and use a single-page document or outline instead. This often makes meetings faster, keeps the discussion direct, and lets people focus on ideas, not visuals.
- *"The Inverted Agenda"*- Place the most complex or high-stakes topic at the beginning, instead of going through

smaller points first. Tackle big decisions when everyone's fresh, leaving minor updates or announcements to the end.

Chapter 7: The Impact of Meeting Culture on Employee Retention

How Meeting Culture Shapes Employee Experience

Management expert Peter Drucker famously said, *"Meetings are a symptom of bad organization. The fewer meetings, the better."* This statement hits hard!

Meeting culture is a direct reflection of an organization's values. It tells employees whether their time is respected, whether leadership is aligned, and whether the company fosters collaboration. When meetings are purposeful, inclusive, and efficient, employees feel valued.

When meetings are poorly managed, however, they signal disrespect for employees' time, leading to frustration and disengagement.

Top talent will scrutinize your company's meeting culture - they'll want proof that their time won't be wasted in endless meetings. That's why having a collective meeting score is so important. Can you demonstrate that employees have time to focus and create, or are they bogged down in back-to-back meetings? Smart people want to work where their contributions matter, not where their calendars are filled with nonessential calls. Your ability to show this data will reflect whether your culture values productivity or bureaucracy.

A survey by Harvard Business Review found that 40% of employees have considered quitting due to meeting overload. In fact, many employees cite excessive or ineffective meetings as a top reason for job dissatisfaction.

Employees report they'd rather do almost anything than sit through another unproductive meeting. Some even say they'd prefer going to the dentist! This speaks volumes about the toll that unnecessary meetings take on motivation and engagement. People crave time for focused work, creative problem-solving, and yes, even mundane tasks - anything that feels more productive than another meeting. It's a clear signal that meeting culture needs a serious overhaul.

Why Millennials and Gen Z Expect Better Meetings

Generational differences in meeting preferences are reshaping how teams work together. Baby Boomers often value in-person meetings, seeing them as essential for building trust and direct communication. Meanwhile, Millennials and Gen Z - who are digital natives - lean toward virtual meetings and asynchronous tools, preferring the efficiency and flexibility they bring.

When these differences go unacknowledged, they can lead to friction. Younger team members may view frequent in-person meetings as outdated and unnecessary, while older colleagues might see digital reliance as too impersonal. Recognizing and bridging these gaps isn't just about accommodating preferences; it's about building a culture where everyone can be productive and fully engaged. The future of work will rely on leaders who can balance these generational insights, creating meeting formats that respect different perspectives and drive real results.

Younger generations - particularly Millennials and Gen Z - have redefined what they expect from work. They are drawn to purpose-driven organizations that align with their values, respect their time, and offer opportunities for meaningful collaboration. These employees are quick to reject companies with outdated meeting practices that waste time or feel bureaucratic.

- A 2022 study from INSEAD found that employees under 35 are 30% more likely to quit jobs with poorly managed meeting cultures than older colleagues. They want meetings to be concise, actionable, and aligned with personal and professional goals.

Research by Professor Thomas Roulet indicates that certain demographics, such as singles, younger employees, and empty nesters, prefer working from the office.

This preference is often driven by the social interactions and structured environment that the office provides, which can be particularly appealing to those seeking to build professional networks or who may have fewer home responsibilities. In contrast, individuals with caregiving duties or those who value flexibility may favor remote work. Understanding these preferences is crucial for organizations aiming to implement effective hybrid work models that cater to diverse employee needs. Working from the office doesn't mean you're looking for more meetings!

Warning Signs of a Toxic Meeting Culture

1. *Meeting Overload:* Employees are forced to attend too many meetings, leaving little time for meaningful work.

2. *Ineffective Discussions:* Meetings drag on without clear outcomes, leading to frustration.

3. *Lack of Inclusion:* Some voices dominate the conversation, while others are ignored.

4. *No Follow-Through:* Decisions made in meetings are not translated into action.

5. *"Surprises."* a vague topic.

Let me clarify what I mean by "Surprises." My friend Rajeeb Dey, an entrepreneur and dear friend, once gave me a piece of advice: sending a vague *"Can we talk?"* message? That's a no-go. It leaves your colleague stressed and distracted, unable to focus on anything else that day - or even the rest of the week - wondering what it might mean. Don't put people in that position. This kind of workplace anxiety is more common than we realize, and it's often avoidable. Great leaders understand that *how* they communicate profoundly impacts team wellbeing. Simple shifts in meeting and messaging styles can change the workplace for the better, creating an environment where people feel informed, valued, and focused.

Here's what great leaders do differently:

1. *They add context upfront:* No more mysterious "quick chat" messages that leave people hanging.

2. *They consider timing:* They avoid sending that "We need to discuss..." email at 11 p.m., understanding that timing matters.
3. *They set clear expectations:* A straightforward "15-min catch-up to go over your project progress" beats vague requests any day.
4. *They're intentionally positive:* Celebrating wins as they happen, instead of saving it all for formal reviews, boosts morale and motivation.
5. *They reduce anxiety, not create it:* They know that when teams feel stressed, productivity drops - so they prioritize clarity and respect in every interaction.

Implementing these (meeting) practices costs nothing, but the impact on team wellbeing is invaluable. Normalizing anxiety-free communication isn't just about what we say - it's about how we make people feel every day.

How Meeting Excellence Builds Trust and Retention

Companies that get meetings right see measurable benefits in employee retention and engagement. When meetings are well-run, employees:

- Feel that their time is respected.
- Experience a sense of accomplishment from collaborative discussions.
- Trust leadership to make efficient decisions.

How Leaders Can Use MQ to Retain Top Talent

1. *Limit Attendance to Relevant Stakeholders:* Over-inviting participants leads to meeting fatigue. Use the RACI framework to invite only those who are essential to the conversation.

2. *Introduce Meeting-Free Days:* Give employees uninterrupted time for deep work by designating certain days as meeting-free.

3. *Foster Psychological Safety:* Create a culture where employees feel comfortable expressing concerns about meeting overload without fear of retribution. Leaders should regularly check in with their teams to ensure meetings are effective and not overwhelming.

4. *Provide Flexible Participation Options:* In hybrid environments, offer asynchronous options for employees who can't attend in real-time. Sharing meeting recordings and summaries ensures everyone stays informed without feeling pressured to attend every meeting.

The Role of Data in Shaping Meeting Culture.

Culture that attracts and retains talent.

- *Eliminate Unnecessary Meetings:* Audit recurring meetings to ensure they still serve a purpose.
- *Limit Meeting Lengths:* Cap meetings to prevent fatigue.
- *Offer Asynchronous Alternatives:* Use tools like Loom for updates that don't require real-time participation.

- *Monitor Meeting Metrics:* Use analytics to track meeting effectiveness and make improvements.
- *Solicit Feedback Regularly:* Create open channels for employees to share their thoughts on meeting culture.

The ROI of a Healthy Meeting Culture

Companies that cultivate a positive meeting culture see:

- *25% higher employee engagement*
- *20% lower turnover rates*
- *30% faster project delivery times*

A strong meeting culture doesn't just improve productivity - it enhances employee well-being and strengthens trust between leadership and teams. In today's competitive job market, companies that prioritize effective meetings will have the edge in attracting and retaining top talent.

Meetings don't have to be a waste of time. In fact, they can be powerful opportunities for collaboration, engagement, and building team culture. Leading meetings effectively is an art that requires "Meeting Intelligence" (MQ) – a blend of emotional, interpersonal, and organizational skills.

- Shift the focus from tasks to relationships - meetings should foster trust and belonging.
- Prioritize engagement by getting to know your team members beyond the meeting room.
- Set clear purposes and agendas to avoid unnecessary meetings and manage time efficiently.

- Continuously learn by observing others and reflecting on your own performance.

Meetings done right can motivate, solve complex problems, and drive meaningful collaboration. It's time to elevate your MQ and lead meetings that matter! Meetings are those little things about "connections" that still matter, and meetings often help build relationships too. An e-mail can't do that. And a Slack message definitely doesn't do that either.

What Email Will Never Replace:

- Checking in on how someone's *really* doing

- Spotting when someone's struggling and stepping in with support

- Letting someone know the difference they make in the project

- Experimenting with better ways to collaborate

The best meetings aren't (just) about status updates - they're about *how* we work together and build trust. They're conversations about being better partners, not just getting things done.

As Thomas Roulet, Associate Professor at Cambridge Judge Business School, highlights the dangers of 'low-quality meetings,' which have become more prevalent, increasing by 7.4% from June 2020 to December 2021. Thomas Roulet defines these meetings as those where participants multitask, get double-booked, or include unnecessary attendees.

His amazing research, featured in MIT Sloan Management Review, reveals that low-quality meetings increase stress, reduce productivity, and diminish work-life balance. The study found that extended workweeks and excessive multitasking correlate with worse outcomes, including increased stress and reduced well-being.

Interestingly, the shift to remote and hybrid work has had mixed effects: while 'focus hours' benefit senior employees working on complex tasks, they can harm junior staff who need more social interaction with their teams. Roulet's work emphasizes the need to rethink meeting practices, moving beyond one-size-fits-all policies for hybrid work, and focusing on meeting quality as a key driver of organizational health. The takeaway? Organizations need to eliminate low-quality meetings to improve engagement and well-being - because in a world of back-to-back calls, meetings should work for people, not against them."

Chapter 8: Asynchronous Communication - A Game-Changer for the Hybrid Era

Meetings drain me - they don't give me energy at all. After a day with 4-5 virtual meetings, I'm exhausted. I pour a lot of energy into everything I do; I just can't "half-ass" a meeting. Because of this, I need structure around how I approach them. How do you feel about meetings? If you're like me, it's essential to find a way to let others know that you prefer more asynchronous work. It can make all the difference in preserving energy and staying productive

What is Asynchronous Communication?

I love this myself so much - asynchronous communication allows participants to exchange information without needing to be present at the same time.

Unlike traditional calls and meetings, where everyone must be available in real-time, asynchronous tools provide the flexibility to engage on their own schedule. This is particularly valuable for remote teams spread across different time zones.

It takes real courage to turn down a meeting and suggest handling it over email, Slack, or chat instead. Some people just can't seem to get enough meetings, but don't be afraid to suggest alternatives - I do it all the time. I simply ask, "Can this be done over email or chat? Do we really need a meeting?" It's not always popular, but it sets an example, and others start to follow suit.

In some company cultures, this approach might not be easy, especially where there's an unspoken belief that productivity means being "visible." But remember, you're challenging that mindset by showing that time spent working - not just being seen - leads to real results.

The Growing Need for Asynchronous Communication

As hybrid work becomes the norm, companies are realizing that real-time meetings are not always necessary. Studies from Stanford University show that asynchronous workflows increase productivity by 20-30%, as employees can work during their most productive hours without interruptions.

Key Benefits of Asynchronous Communication

1. *Increased Flexibility:* Employees can engage at their own convenience, leading to better work-life balance and reduced burnout.

2. *Reduced Meeting Overload:* Teams can reserve real-time meetings for critical discussions and use asynchronous tools for updates or status reports.

3. *Better Time Zone Coverage:* Asynchronous communication ensures that teams across different regions can stay aligned without forcing anyone to attend meetings outside their working hours.

Many workers like asynchronous work, since it allows them to squeeze work in between tasks like running errands or tending to childcare. Also, remote and asynchronous work are distinct but complementary approaches. While remote work can still follow traditional 9-to-5 schedules with synchronous Zoom check-ins, asynchronous work allows employees to complete tasks on their own timelines, without the need for immediate responses. This flexibility fosters deep work by minimizing interruptions and reducing meeting fatigue.

With asynchronous communication, documentation becomes essential, making it easier to onboard new employees and ensure transparency around decisions. Teams across different time zones or those managing family responsibilities benefit most, as work-life balance improves without the pressure of fixed hours. However, asynchronous work isn't for everyone and requires thoughtful implementation to align with both individual and team needs.

When to Use Asynchronous vs. Synchronous Communication

Leaders with high MQ know that not every conversation requires a meeting. Here's how to decide between the two:

- Use Synchronous Communication for:
    - Brainstorming sessions
    - High-stakes decision-making
    - Conversations that require immediate feedback
- Use Asynchronous Communication for:

- Status updates and progress reports
- Sharing documents or presentations
- Gathering feedback over time

Tools for Effective Asynchronous Communication

1. *Loom:* Record video updates that team members can watch on their own time.
   - Use Case: Instead of a Monday morning meeting, send a Loom video outlining the team's priorities for the week.

2. *Notion or Google Docs:* Share collaborative documents where participants can add comments and suggestions asynchronously.
   - Use Case: Draft a project plan and invite team members to provide input over the next few days.

3. *Slack or Microsoft Teams:* Use chat channels for quick updates and questions that don't require a meeting.
   - Use Case: Set up a Slack channel for daily project updates instead of holding a daily stand-up.

How to Integrate Asynchronous Communication into Your Organization

1. *Start Small:* Begin by replacing one recurring meeting with an asynchronous update. Monitor how it impacts productivity and engagement.

2. *Set Clear Expectations:* Define response times for asynchronous communications to avoid delays. For

example, team members should respond to project updates within 24 hours.

3. *Use Video Strategically:* Recorded videos offer a more personal touch than emails or documents. Use them to convey complex information or provide context.

4. *Follow Up with Summaries:* After sharing asynchronous updates, send a brief summary to ensure everyone is aligned.

Overcoming Challenges with Asynchronous Communication

While asynchronous tools offer flexibility, they can also create challenges if not managed properly. Leaders must:

- *Avoid Information Overload:* Keep asynchronous updates concise and focused.

- *Maintain Engagement:* Encourage team members to participate actively in discussions, even if they aren't happening in real time.

- *Monitor Progress:* Use tools like Trello or Asana to track action items from asynchronous updates.

Checklist: Best Practices for Asynchronous Communication

- *Choose the Right Tools:* Select platforms that align with your team's needs.

- *Set Response Expectations:* Define clear timelines for replies.

- *Keep Updates Concise:* Focus on essential information.

- *Combine with Synchronous Meetings:* Use live meetings only when necessary.

- *Monitor and Adjust:* Continuously assess the effectiveness of asynchronous communication and make improvements as needed.

The ROI of Asynchronous Communication

Organizations that integrate asynchronous communication report:

- *30% fewer meetings per week*
- *20% higher employee satisfaction*
- *Faster project completion times*

Asynchronous communication isn't just a trend - it's a core strategy for the future of work. Leaders who master it will create flexible, high-performing teams that can collaborate seamlessly across time zones and geographies.

Leaders who embrace asynchronous tools will not only reduce meeting fatigue but also enhance productivity and improve employee well-being. By integrating asynchronous workflows, organizations can stay aligned without sacrificing flexibility - giving them a competitive edge in the future of work. BUT - asynchronous work offers freedom, but it blurs the line between work and personal life - making it too easy to check emails at midnight. It can also lead to isolation, with employees missing the instant feedback and social cues of real-time interaction.

More autonomy brings more responsibility, shifting the burden to employees to stay informed and manage tasks independently. While this setup builds trust, it can also trigger micromanagement as employers try to monitor productivity remotely. The challenge is balancing freedom with connection - giving employees space to work while keeping them aligned with the team.

Chapter 9: Leveraging Technology to Enhance Meeting Intelligence

The Rise of Technology in Modern Meetings

Technology has become a game-changer in how we meet, automating processes, driving engagement, and offering new ways to collaborate in real time.

AI-powered tools, collaborative platforms, and data analytics are essential for running efficient meetings. Leaders who embrace these tools enhance their Meeting Intelligence (MQ), creating smarter, faster, and more effective meetings. The future of meetings belongs to organizations that understand how to leverage technology not only to save time but also to foster deeper connections across distributed teams. As work becomes increasingly digital, leaders must harness technology to streamline operations, capture insights, and drive productivity.

> *"Meetings are indispensable when you don't want to anything."*
>
> **John Kenneth Galbraith**

This story serves as a reminder that leadership titles don't always guarantee effective meeting skills:

"Simply put, my manager schedules WAY too many meetings! We meet every single day for between 60 and 90 minutes, with no agenda, and not enough updates to fill the time, yet she insists on continuing to schedule them, and drag out the meeting for the entire scheduled duration. I typically give 5-10 minutes of updates, I generally ping her when I have questions or need anything from her, so the rest of the meeting time is spent in utter silence. She refuses to turn on her video during the calls, so it's impossible to read her body language during the silent periods. I've tried the "well, that's all I have for today, I'll let you know if I need anything else," but she doesn't take the bait and we end up staying on the line.

The other thing is that there is no set meeting time. She schedules these the night before (if not, the day of) and it makes it difficult to plan my days.

How can I:

A. Politely imply that we don't need a daily meeting, especially not for an hour?

B. Ask for a standing meeting?"

What advice would you give her?

Chapter 10: Frameworks for Meeting Success - Practical Tools for Leaders

Why Frameworks Matter in Effective Meetings

Frameworks provide the structure and clarity needed to run efficient and productive meetings. Without clear guidelines, meetings can easily become chaotic or unproductive. Leaders with high MQ use proven frameworks to align teams, assign roles, and track progress.

Frameworks for Meeting Excellence

The 5 Ws Framework (Who, What, When, Where, Why):

This simple but powerful framework aligns participants by clearly defining the **purpose and scope** of the meeting. Every meeting should address:

- **Who** needs to attend?
- **What** will be discussed?
- **When** will it take place?
- **Where** will it happen (in-person or virtual)?
- **Why** are we meeting?

These questions are lifesavers, guiding everyone to stay on track by answering a few essential questions upfront. First, think about **WHO** actually needs to be there, fewer people often make for better conversations, and no one likes to sit through a meeting that could have been a quick update. Then there's the **WHAT**: set a clear agenda. Vague topics lead to meandering discussions, so let's define what we're tackling ahead of time. Personally, I do not join meetings with more than 7 people.

WHEN we meet also matters, a meeting late Friday afternoon? Not ideal. Aim for times that work for everyone's energy, not just the calendar. The **WHERE** question is key, too. Are we meeting in person, or will this be virtual? Either way, it should feel meaningful and not like a formality. And finally, there's the all-important **WHY** - if there's no clear purpose, is this meeting really necessary? Sometimes, a quick email or chat message can get the job done faster and more efficiently. In short, having these answers turns meetings from dreaded time-sinks into intentional, productive moments. And trust me, as someone who's spent plenty of time in every kind of meeting, this approach keeps everyone's sanity intact.

I honestly think it shouldn't be so easy to book someone's time - whether it's on Outlook or any calendar app - without first answering a few basic questions. Inviting people to meetings shouldn't be a quick click-and-send; it should actually take some thought. Right now, it's way too easy to just pick a time and push send, cluttering up calendars without a second thought. Greg McKeown, who wrote *Essentialism*, nails it - being more intentional with our time could save everyone a lot of energy and help us focus on what really matters.

The OKR Framework (Objectives and Key Results):

OKRs help focus meetings on measurable outcomes. Leaders align each meeting with specific objectives, ensuring that discussions contribute directly to the company's goals.

How to Implement Frameworks Effectively

1. *Choose the Right Framework:* Select a framework based on the meeting's purpose. For decision-making, use the RACI model; for brainstorming, try the 5Ws framework.

2. *Train Facilitators:* Ensure managers understand how to apply these frameworks to their meetings.

3. *Monitor Progress:* Use OKRs to measure the effectiveness of meetings over time and make adjustments as needed.

Chapter 11: Your Role in Shaping the Future of Meetings

The Future of Work Belongs to Leaders with High MQ

In a world where time is the most valuable resource, leaders who master the art of meetings will stand out. Meeting Intelligence (MQ) isn't just a skill - it's a competitive advantage. Leaders who innovate meeting practices will attract top talent, retain employees, and foster a culture of trust and collaboration.

How You Can Lead the Way

1. *Be a Role Model for Meeting Excellence:* Show others how to design purposeful, engaging meetings. Your behavior will set the tone for the entire organization.

2. *Continuously Improve:* Use feedback and analytics to refine your meeting practices over time. High MQ leaders are always learning and adapting.

Call to Action: Lead the Future of Meetings

The future of work belongs to those who challenge the status quo. By mastering MQ, you can create meetings that are more than just conversations - they become platforms for alignment, trust, and innovation. Start by applying the principles and frameworks in this book and inspire others to do the same.

Chapter 12: Conclusion - Your Journey to Master Meeting Intelligence (MQ)

Bringing It All Together

Mastering Meeting Intelligence (MQ) isn't just about running better meetings - it's about transforming how we work, collaborate, and lead. In this book, we've explored the foundations of MQ, shared actionable frameworks, and showcased real-world examples of companies that have redefined their meeting culture.

But the journey doesn't end here. Applying these principles in your own work is where the real magic happens. Whether you're leading a team, consulting with clients, or preparing for your next startup, the way you design and run meetings will shape your success.

Call to Action - Shape the Future of Work

The future of work belongs to those who challenge the status quo. Meetings, when done right, are powerful tools for alignment, innovation, and progress. As you move forward, I encourage you to:

- *Apply the principles of MQ* to every meeting you lead.
- *Share these insights* with your teams and clients.

- *Inspire others* to rethink meetings as strategic opportunities.

This is your moment to become a meeting expert and a leader in the future of work. Whether you're running a startup, leading a team, or consulting with organizations, your ability to design and facilitate great meetings will set you apart.

Meetings are often seen as time sinks, but they don't have to be. Done right, they can become powerful tools for fostering relationships, building trust, and driving team performance. Research shows that 70% of meetings hinder productivity due to inefficiency, but meetings can also offer a unique opportunity to foster collaboration, develop a sense of belonging, and shape team culture.

The key takeaway? Meetings aren't just about getting work done - they're about creating spaces where people feel connected and heard. The most effective leaders shift their focus from task management to relationship-building, recognizing that strong connections lead to better outcomes. Junior employees, in particular, thrive when they feel part of a collective effort, which makes well-structured meetings invaluable for engagement.

To achieve this, leaders need to develop what we call Meeting Intelligence (MQ) - the ability to run meetings that are inclusive, purposeful, and engaging. MQ goes beyond Emotional Intelligence (EQ) or Wellbeing Intelligence (WBQ), combining interpersonal skills with organizational awareness. Effective meetings require not just managing time and content but also preparing the environment and relationships to create meaningful dialogue.

Great meetings aren't just about delivering updates - they're about connecting the right people at the right time with the right purpose. It's not just about following an agenda but fostering a culture of engagement, collaboration, and personal connection. In hybrid work environments, meetings become even more crucial as opportunities to bridge physical and emotional distance among team members.

The best meetings achieve three things:

1. *Motivate the team:* They reinforce a shared identity and boost morale.

2. *Allocate tasks effectively:* They ensure buy-in by aligning tasks with the right people.

3. *Facilitate creative problem-solving:* They encourage brainstorming and decision-making, reducing blind spots and cognitive bias.

Meetings need clear purpose, structure, and follow-through. Leaders who master the art of meetings understand that preparation is essential - whether it's crafting the agenda, building relationships with participants, or ensuring everyone understands why they are involved. They also learn to manage time effectively and know when to move conversations forward to avoid unproductive tangents.

The goal is to transform meetings from a dreaded obligation into a valuable part of team culture. Meetings should leave participants energized and motivated, not drained. Every meeting should have a clear purpose, engage the right participants, and result in actionable outcomes that everyone understands and supports.

The best products and services, the ones that genuinely respect and empower humanity, are born from a diversity of perspectives and insights. Meetings give cross-functional teams the critical platform to share ideas, challenge assumptions, and align on what truly matters to the customer.

You have a unique role in life - at work - you're not just a participant but a steward of a collaborative environment(s). Meetings are the intersection of customer-focused thinking and innovation, where ideas evolve into solutions that make a difference. In meetings, you (should) set the tone, create a culture that values psychological safety, encourages fresh perspectives, and keeps customer-centricity at the core.

Time is limited, and the demands are high, but it's the right meetings that drive an organization forward. When done well, meetings don't just maintain momentum, they're the engine that propels teams to build products that align with a larger purpose. It's about fostering an environment where everyone's expertise is valued, and where insights lead to impact. My friend, and bestselling author McKeown has said that 99% of meetings are a waste of time, and I agree.

The future of meetings is human-centric. With AI and rapid change reshaping the workplace, the role of the leader becomes more important than ever. Leaders must cultivate genuine relationships and foster mental well-being, ensuring meetings remain spaces where people feel connected and valued. A meeting isn't just a task - it's a moment to build trust, spark innovation, and nurture belonging.

Consider to implement the rule of 3 X 3: if there is a leader of the team that everyone looks to for answers, or if there is someone that tends to dominate discussions, do not allow them to talk until 3 other people have spoken or until 3 minutes have passed, whichever is later. Have systems in place to make your meetings the most inclusive and productive ones. Running a meeting is a lot like conducting an orchestra - it takes practice, self-awareness, and a commitment to constant improvement. The real pros make meetings that not only get things done but also build a culture where people thrive and teams truly succeed.

The "3Cs" - communication, connection, and celebration - are a powerful way to make meetings meaningful (even if we're not sure who came up with them originally):

- *Communication:* Keep things open and clear so everyone feels informed and part of the conversation.
- *Connection:* Create a space where real relationships form and collaboration happens naturally.
- *Celebration:* Take a moment to recognize wins, big or small - it keeps morale high and purpose front and center.

When you combine the 3Cs with the PERMA model, you're creating an environment where people feel engaged every time they show up. And instead of asking if your meetings are "great," ask if they're worth everyone's time. Not every meeting has to be amazing, but it should always feel worth it.

To start transforming your meetings tomorrow, begin with intention. Don't schedule a meeting just because it's routine or expected. Instead, ask yourself, "What's the purpose, and what's the outcome we need?" Craft your agenda to focus on those essentials and invite only the people who truly need to be there. Begin with small changes - shorten the meeting by 15 minutes, end with clear action items, or try a quick "silent start" where everyone reads the agenda first. These small shifts build momentum.

Now, if you face pushback from colleagues, remember that changing meeting culture can feel disruptive. Explain that these adjustments aren't about restricting voices or reducing collaboration - they're about freeing everyone's time for work that matters. When someone resists, frame it as a shared experiment: "Let's try this for a week or two and see if it improves outcomes."

You'll likely find that even skeptical colleagues soon realize the benefits and may even adopt these practices themselves.

With effort and intention, meetings can become the beating heart of organizational success. The question now is: How will you transform your meetings? Will they be just another obligation, or will they become a tool for meaningful leadership? The choice is yours.

Let's Connect and Continue the Conversation

I'd love to hear your thoughts on this book and how you're applying MQ in your work. You can reach me through my website www.soulaima.com or book me as a speaker or workshop facilitator through BigSpeak Speakers Bureau.

If you've found the strategies in *The Meeting Black Belt* valuable and want to take your skills to the next level, consider enrolling in **The Meeting Black Belt™ Certificate Program.** This comprehensive training equips you with advanced tools, live coaching, and practical insights to transform your meetings into powerful, results-driven sessions. It's the perfect next step for mastering Meeting Intelligence (MQ) and earning a credential that sets you apart as a leader as well as a certificate that elevates your CV. Learn more at soulaima.com under the "Programs" tab.

Let's continue to transform meetings together and create a future of work where every conversation counts.

A special shoutout to Thomas Roulet - my brilliant partner in all things meeting related. Together, we explore how to eliminate the bad ones and create more high-quality, impactful meetings. Thomas is a Professor of Organizational Sociology and Leadership at the Judge Business School, University of Cambridge, and co-founder of the King's Entrepreneurship Lab at King's College, Cambridge.

www.ingramcontent.com/pod-product-compliance
Lightning Source LLC
Chambersburg PA
CBHW070115230526
45472CB00004B/1260